For Barba

35

poems, prose, images

Best Wishes

Paul Robert Mullen

35

poems, prose, images

Paul Robert Mullen

Coyote Creek Books | San José | California

Printed in the United States of America

ISBN-13: 978-1-946647-19-1
25 24 23 22 21 20 19 18   1 2 3 4 5 6 7

Cover design © 2018 by Jan McCutcheon
Cover photo © 2018 by Caleb Wilkinson
Back cover photo © 2018 by Derek Sykes
Back cover photo of author © 2018 by Lei Li Xian

Published by Coyote Creek Books
www.coyotecreekbooks.com

for
you
and for me
and for anybody else
who may be
this way inclined

primitive cool

also by Paul Robert Mullen

curse this blue raincoat (2017)
testimony (2018)

35

crossroads in winter

this age has brought me

        to the crossroads

winter staring down at me

        with intrigue . . .

contents 35 contents

preface

35

35 years.

 35 poems.

35 times putting pen to paper.

 35 fewer monkeys on my back.

35 reasons to wonder.

 35 cool images to ponder.

 35 once . . . . .

 forever.

"age is a hell of a price to pay for wisdom"

George Carlin

made in china

she
is not even
    a
cheap replacement of
    you

she
is just skin and bone

    empty

and
i
    am just
        the meat

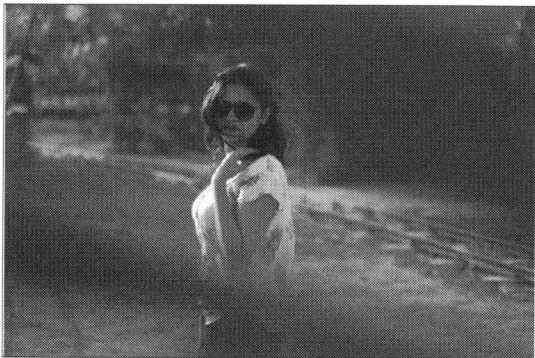

you

someone to love

you lie
naked as an x-ray
half
illuminated
    by
      the early morning sun

and i wait
in the doorway
exploring the contours
    on your back

7:32am –

not even
the tribulation
    could break this silence

early morning sun

a miracle

when i look at you
i think it's a miracle that we were
      put on earth
in the same space
at the same time. all the years
and decades
and centuries
         that could have been chosen for us
all the places
on this vast planet
         that we might have grown
all the billions of lives
entwined
that we have waded through
to touch skin;
       our lives
       our time
       our chromosomes aligned

we sit
across tables, across nations
across universes
across smiles –
       two temporary skins
         eternally bound

a *miracle*

8   35

the small hours

at night
        i burn for you

what do *you* burn for?

burn

flavours of you

you are the
        fresh mint
in
my mojito

a little spicy, slightly
        sour
to the
        touch

curious
at the very least

the more you touch
        my lips
the
drunker
        i become

curious at the very least

twilight

i
stayed in the sun too long
that summer

the summer
the crops withered
but
we blossomed, growing together
on the dusty plain
beside
the airport

and grandma
said my neck had
turned a lovely colour
which
made you laugh
that guttural, juvenile giggle
with your dimples on show

and i fell in love
that summer
though i didn't know what love was
or what joys
terrors
ecstasies
humiliations

it could bring

you see
           then
love
was simply seeing your smile
your grace
in the late afternoon
           sun

oh
           mother

if only

grace

to love in stages

i carved pieces of myself
to fit
the shape
you needed me to be
      but
you said my art was
drab

i chiselled at my edges
so you
might give me a second look
pleaded
with the stars to align
so we might
share more than just
      a passing glance

i gave
my entire waking thoughts
to you

      like i really had a choice

comeback

what is this shit?
                    you say, throwing
          the pile of poems
          at me
          that you found in the drawer

                              what kind of man writes this shit?

the kind of man that lives with a woman like you
          i say
gathering up the papers
noticing
the clock
          strike
               6.15 am

voluntary exit

sometimes i think about how nice it would be
    to get off this planet –

post-ejaculation
    watching the breaking news
    teenage balding
the inability to refuse

travelling on buses
    sunday mornings coming down
    donald trump – leader of the free world
this twisted rat-race
        merry-go-round

american sitcoms
    listening to blood-boiling canteen clitter-clatter
    putrid drains and dog-shit stains
mars bars cooked
        in heart-attack batter

mothers-in-law
    low-budget economy plane seating
    minimum wage in provincial towns
school bullies
    handing out
        a routine beating

dentists, loan-sharks
    terrorism, fundamentalism
    standing room on jam-packed subways
fallen angels and evangelism

Elvis dead at 42
    the sickly smell of hospital sweat
    homophobic ignorance
        forever stuck in mounds of debt

cockroach slime
        the k.k.k
    circle jerking, supercilious smirking
never knowing what to say

cheese and onion wotsits
    blowing up history
    monks burning at the crossroads
insincere reverie

6.15am in winter
    the horror of teeny-bop-pop
    touring temples for the sake of it
the diet that starts tomorrow
        because you just can't stop

corned beef and crème caramel
    brexit, cancer,
        justin beiber

bungee jump numbness on a gambling island
the realisation that
you have to leave her

farts with no windows
homicide when walking the dog
backstreets in thailand at 11pm
the plane crash death of rock and roll
when they should never
have taken off in fog

rap music
blackheads, cysts, right-wingers
child abusers in the senate
extra-marital sticky fingers

napalm bombs
surrogate childhoods
doubting yourself
just before asking for a date
strange noises at dusk coming
from the woods

extinction, body odour
cheating tuk-tuk taxi drivers
a hair in your food
that knocks you sick
massive bird eating spiders

crack-house sex
  senseless genocide
  avocado shaped heads
serial killers offering anyone, *every*one a free ride

bum notes in a symphony
  decapitation of one's epiphany
  abandonment and social class systems
the futile, never-ending
    quest to be free

green with envy
  wikileaks
  the iphone four-hundred and fifty-seven
the tragic kid at school who reeks

snapped string in a searing solo
  devils in my head
  families skating on thin ice
chemical weapons
    and the living dead

soldiers coming home in boxes
  mothers crippled, slumped in arms
  fat-cat politicians
    faking grief and remorse
twisted rhetoric, false alarms

and then

       the question nobody has
the time to consider:

what if this idea of fake news

               is just fake news?

voluntary exit

Paul Robert Mullen   21

in chains

i have wanderlust

i guess i need you to know

it's no use
keeping me under lock and key
putting blinkers on me
pulling me away when someone
                new enters the frame

i'll always break free
when you believe you have
            my every limb
                    my every whim
            my everything
in chains

i could say i'm sorry
            but
then
i'd have to mean it

wanderlust

Paul Robert Mullen

fantasy

maybe
       the only time
i
really
       love you
is when
       i
am between your legs

maybe
       the only time
you
really
       love me
is when
       i'm gone

no use

i
tried to heal you
by
fucking you

but

fucking you
              opened
wounds
you never knew
           you had

nobody ever really knows

maybe a terrible, aching death
    awaits me

maybe i will die in my sleep
    aged 93

maybe the stars will implode
    and catapult us all toward serenity

maybe the trash collectors of the world
    will blow up wall street

maybe Paul McCartney will
    live forever

maybe you will fall
    and split the thin ice of modern life

maybe i will pick you up
    or maybe i won't

maybe a colony of bigfoot will emerge
    from the fantasies of cryptozoology and shake
        the foundations

maybe we will scream
    until silence reigns

35

maybe twilight will follow dawn
    and rape routine
        of all its repetitious rules

maybe the losers
    will come through and win

maybe we will start again
    primitive cool, pure survival

maybe i will drink this tea
    steaming green, hibiscus tint
            before it reaches lukewarm

maybe the insane greed that pours blood & bone
    into marble and stone
    will surrender itself, hands aloft
        on every street

maybe we will rock'n'roll

maybe the wild-eyed-wanderers of the world will return home
    to find everything is nothing;
            it was all just reverie

maybe the sweeping technological advances that turn the streets
    cold
            and gather the masses into the deep
                insane pits of addiction will combust

spontaneously

    maybe us and them
       will become one

maybe we will walk the corridors
    of the future
    together
       fearless

maybe they will love
    and i will love
    and you will love
       and love
         will reign supreme

just
    maybe

maybe we will walk the corridors of the future together

nameless

i can swallow your lies
and though
they wedge themselves in my intestines
tumble in my gut
i grip the walls until the pain
        subsides
smile
and invite you in
        like i don't know

you swirl your spoon around
the china cup, clinking unnecessarily
        and i feel the furnace
          pressing at my temples
but i squeeze my fists into my cheeks
     squeeze, squeeze, squeeze
my face burning
eyes faking placidity
some bullshit about the witch at work

           "fucking *horror*," you scratch
from the pit of
your throat, flicking your wrist
        at the air
like
you are swatting the truth
        away

and i tolerate hours of your
shit
    you lying cunt

      but i cannot do what i really
      aught to do;
            smack you in the mouth
            light you up
                put you through glass
            burn your house down

            i
            just sit and swallow
            it all, like i've always
                done – like i'll
                    always do

because some of us are just made that way

buried

the day you left
heading out at dusk on your
                          final road to excess
i waited
until i was sure you were long gone

i took a spade

when the dawn hours
began letting in a little light
i dug up my heart, which had lay buried
at the back of the yard
                        for years
shook it off, placed it
in my camel-skin coat pocket

i carried it with me
for a whole lifetime
                        though it
didn't start beating
again for years. it took me by surprise
        one day
in a supermarket queue, when i felt the slight
dramatic surge
            of electricity
in that deep-purple leathery pouch
of atriums

it didn't feel better
                    straight away
knowing that now
i was officially alive

                that took years, too

i did notice, however
that people looked at me differently

        look at you, they'd say. *such colour in your cheeks!*

        please don't look at me, i'd reply.

lots of things changed
after my heart started beating again

sometimes i felt the need
to cry. often i would feel overcome
with affection for something – often animals
or sometimes
            someone i didn't even know

            i found
that i desired people; an altogether peculiar
emotion for someone
like me
            numb for so long

i stroked dogs and enjoyed it, even if they
shunned my attentions

your name came up
in conversation now and again
        (since now i was even communicating)
and i heard
all sorts of terrible things.
        you were out of your mind
smack-drowned, blow-torched, tanked-up drunk
        on the streets
running with the hunted
        at claustrophobic speed

there were days
when i considered putting my heart
back in the ground
covering it with soil
        asking the birds
to bear witness
                but i never did

i kept it beating
                ever so softly
in the pocket
of my camel-skin coat
walking the streets like a normal
guy with a normal life
in a normal state of mind, in a standard

three-piece suit,
                    9 to 5 smile

there were times
when i brushed my hair. took a shave. debated
in my mind whether to
do something fun
at the weekend, or surrender
under a bridge downtown, across town, *any* town
where civilised eyes
                    would never go

pariah

don't
put a 'y' on the end of my name
like you're entitled to
my affection

don't
categorise me
trivialise me
objectify me
call me your friend

don't
use me as your means
      to
make amends

don't
talk about me
      talk to me
compliment me
try to manipulate me

don't
visit me
and make it sound like you're
doing me a favour

don't
play the music i love
through the walls; it'll always be
my favourite
not *ours*

don't
justify your creepiness
with gifts
and material advances
          because
no amount of money can repair
the damage
you've left in your wake

don't
call me / text me / facebook me
instagram me / wechat me
          skype me
or go through others
          to
                    settle scores with me

don't
ever use the term
'brother'
when referring
          to me –
if your blood was my blood

i'd cut myself
until it had drained away

don't
imitate me, praise me
berate me
make an example of me
taunt me
surprise me
blow smoke up my ass
               or celebrate me

and
don't
      ever
mistake
'me'
     for 'we'

        again

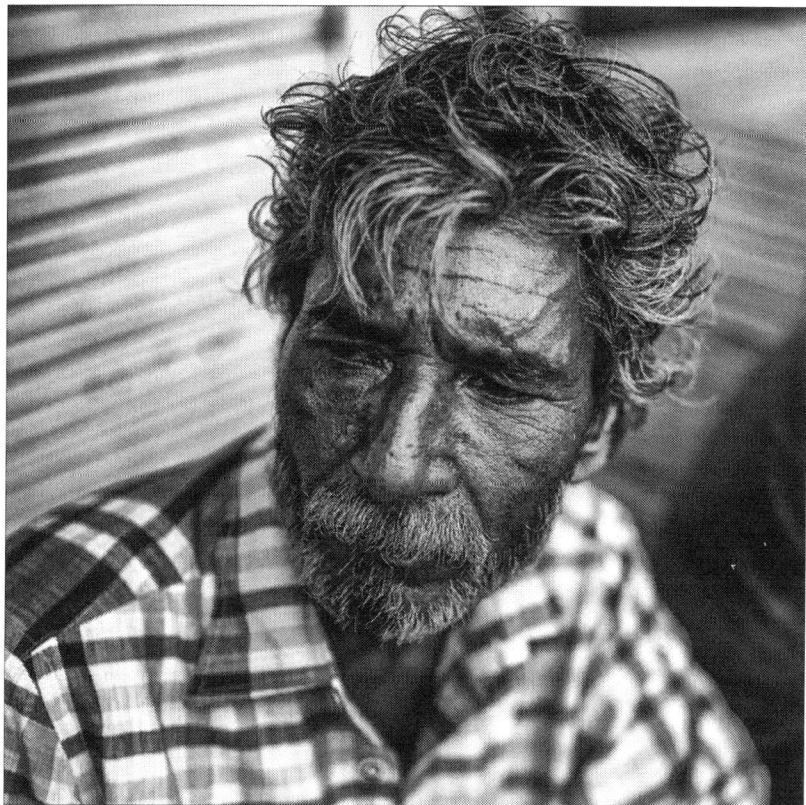

pariah

if i had my time again

i kept sweeping you
under
the mat
like a small pile
            of dust
i couldn't
quite bring myself to
        rid of

i guess i knew
you'd come back, quietly
        purposefully
so i got on with my humdrum existence
without
a thought for you

        sweeping
                waiting
        sweeping
                waiting

then all of a sudden
        you
                didn't come back –

        i turned the mat
upside down

for days

looking

searching

craving something
        i
never knew i
        needed

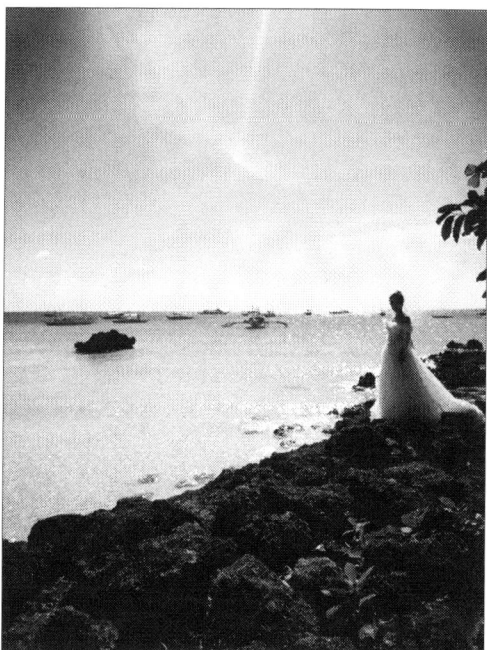

constant craving

erudition

one day i may learn to let go
of
the things
i cannot
     control
because
this lockjaw
     grip
through night and day
is
leaving me
     weak

erudition

35

another night in a dying city

over

and i'm walking home alone
    again

midnight
        long gone
streets deserted bar
the occasional
        drone
of distant taxis on
        the main roads humming
like wasps in summer
returning
the surrendered, hen-pecked, exhausted
        suicidal
  to their cold
      marital beds

no such (bad?) luck
  for me

instead, the hiccup
      of an overloaded gut
    and the fog of uncertain
  thoughts
      repeating

in the cool late-night
breeze

needing voices
       fearing voices

and
i've only got a t-shirt on
because a crowded pub is always warm
       even in winter
the breath
of a hundred husky voices
bouncing off the walls
cheap talk
       drama
the bitch at work
       gym guy with the new wheels
the queers shedding tears
       at the funeral
the slut with the fake tan
       the price
           of being worth something
the hot young mom
       in the school yard
          (are they *really* fake tits?)
       the jock with the big cock
trump and co.
the trump show
trump this, trump that

trump's a genius
trump's a twat
whose is the
   aston martin parked outside?
George Michael dying
Prince dying
Leonard Cohen dying
   seemingly everyone dying

and i cant help
but
remember the times
my mother would say
   "don't go out without your coat
      or you'll regret it later on"
or the times
my father would say
nothing
  at all
unless he was told to

   "but i don't *need* to," i'd say
    "i'm only going to be in a taxi and then
       straight in the bar"

and then that uncompromising stare

   "put it *on*"

in my mind
the streets are on fire
and
the madhouses and the brothels and the squats
        and the nightclub side-alleys
        supermarket carparks
cemeteries, dormitories, taxi ranks, junkyards
        they're all
                up in flames

though
the streets are numb
tonight
        every night
everywhere
you look
        curtains drawn
                        lights off
        gates closed
        eyes closed
        lives closed

rapid movements counting sheep
the occasional gang
        in fear
of their own shadows

        even the cats are quiet
they've fucked themselves

into oblivion
scratched their way
      into a million feline dreams

and it's like
all my urges
have been switched on
      at once
a warehouse of wicked
imaginings
      suddenly drowned in light

but
the reality is worse than
the sum
      of my fantasies;
      my un-kissed lips drowned
         in bad oil
the stench of
      rancid, dripping fried chicken
lingering
      in my armpits
one of the last signs
of the night
      one of the first signs of
         exquisite loneliness

the minutes
move faster than my feet

and i can feel dawn creeping up
behind me
    like a halloween surprise

another 4am
festering
with the world wide web
    and
the memories of a fading youth
spinning the wheel
        round and round
     and round
     and
       round

dying city

hangover

last night
i drank my fill

today
i'm aching still

another night in the lion's den

running down a dream
and yet
needlessly becoming

the kill

precision

Paul Robert Mullen

my last friday night out for a while

somebody laughs, tells a
dead baby joke
  and it's *him*
everyone avoiding the wild glare
of social ineptness
   inappropriateness
and
he screams
    "come on, fuckers! what's up with you?"

the collective howl
of disappointment breaks the tension
hanging in the air
like exhaust fumes –
   england
have missed another penalty
   choked again
another chance at glory
resigned to mocking headlines

   "useless bastards!" someone shouts

and the slams of multiple glasses
clatter the bar for the final
time
   that evening

the final whistle
brings
        exodus
and the pub is down
to five

        "this shithole got nothin' goin' on!" he shouts

and i feel sure
he is
goading a reaction
inciting me to act
        but
i don't want to act, i just
want to drink
i don't even want to talk
since people are
        diabolical

        "pipe down, X," the landlord says

in a voice that's heard it all before
and X's baseball cap
is pulled down almost over his eyes
just a dark grey shadow
underneath the peak

        "keep your voice down," the landlord adds

pointing, warning
and this guy just keeps peering
at me
like a hungry wolf
so i turn my back, push a coin
into the jukebox
        press some numbers
take a breath

        "what's this *shit*?"
sneering
            and i can feel the heat
under my collar, the moisture on
the back of my neck
nobody
        else looking up
nobody
        else wanting any part of the pot
        beginning to boil
and i just
can't help it
                i look up
and there he is
staring me down, the time barely
                    8pm
me, hardly halfway
through my life

        "you into this *shit*?" he snarls, and now i know he wants me

the eyes of the few left
dancing
in their heads

"yes."

      "faggot," he snipes
                emptying his glass
                      calling in another –

      "pull the tap!" he demands, drumming on
                the cider

and the landlord eyes me
with that uncertainty
reserved
for those who wait, braced
for
worst case scenarios
but business
      is slack; every sale adds to the
coppers
so he pulls the tap
and my heart skips a beat

i feel the shadows
      shifting
X
striding towards me

and my muscles tense, my mind squeezing
                    at my brain
i prepare, steady
but i don't know why
          i just *do*
and
suddenly my personal space
is steamy, claustrophobic, as he edges me
          out of the light
smelling stale
cigarette smoke and sweat and a whole heap of
          booze and regret

click, click, click, click, click

five coins into the slot
a message
to the pub that he is top dog
          and
we'd be listening to his tunes
for the rest of the night
whether
we like it or not

          "skip this fag *shit*!" he shouts
                    to anyone who will listen

          "skip it!" he bellows again
                    at the landlord

who debates his next move
but figures it's easier
just to skip it
so he leans in and presses the button
and i feel my blood rise
ten degrees
                purple rain decimated
and the old guy
next to me starts to move
                sensing trouble
puts down his half-finished bitter
slips on a cashmere, stained beige
shuffles out;
                he wants
exit before the storm
                and i cant blame him
                since the clouds are gathering
                thick

                "ever had a song dedicated
                        to ya?" he scowls

and the landlord
switches off the tv, turns off the lights
in the snug
where only the ghosts of
hours passed
hang

"yes," i lie
           and something
is happening to my eyes
maybe
they are drying up
maybe
they are filling up
maybe
they are blowing up

he slams his pint glass on the bar
but the landlord shakes
his head
           "no more," he says, "no more."
and i see
the change in X before
he realises it in himself; a kind of
glass-eyed trance
chest puffed out
arms ready for the war
           he is still stuck in

           "pull another pint," he says evenly

and something about the calm
in his voice
           clatters in my brain
           like a knife
                 inside a tin can

"i wont tell you again," the landlord asserts
      "we're *done* here."

and it feels
like someone's finger is resting
in the pin
ready to pull, ready to hurl
the air even thicker than oxtail soup
so thick that it's hard
to breathe

      "well i aint leaving 'till i've had my fill,"
         he snarls
and
i just can't hold my
mouth

      "he said no more," i snap

and
the eyes of a thousand
angry dreams
fix themselves on me like a barrel
      on a target

      "*what* did you say?"

the heat on my neck turns cold –
it's that sinister tone

of calm
again

the silence before the thunder

the
cool before the crack

"you heard what i said"

my voice brave
braver than i feel
and he stirs
shuffles from foot to foot
slouches
then straightens against the
jukebox
smokestack lightning bulging
in his pupils
fists clenched like combat units
and those seconds
feel like months in a jungle
everybody stone-cold
still

only the thump
of
my heart
against my ribs

it's been fifteen years since
i've had to fight
and
my arms are starting to tingle

            "i've eaten guys like you for supper
                all my life,"
                            he whispers, shark-faced grin
and
it's all come down to this
all of my days and my weeks and my years
all of my petty teenage fears
the smoke and the sun
the times i've mistaken danger for fun
the sweat and endless
amounts of student debt
        the winter mornings shovelling shit;

it's all come
            to this

"that's enough, X," the landlord says

and it's the stillness
of everything
that's really getting to me
ramping
        up the temperature
his steely eyes fixed

on my chest
nothing
but impenetrable moments of calm
standing between
me
and a full-scale

        shit-show

"i wont fight you," i say
      a quiver in
            my resolve
and
he laughs
      and laughs
and laughs
until
the hairs stand up on the back
of my neck

nobody moves
nobody
    dares

    "you know i've killed men . . ."

slurring
twitching
    pushing the buttons

and the room
is spinning, shaking, taking off
            like a plane
out of control
and there's a howl
and a flash of light
a million recollections screaming past my retinas
            like a bullet train
                        fizzing through blinding sun
and i don't know whose face is whose
or whose pain i'm swallowing
or whose voice is wailing
or whose nails are breaking
            flesh
or what the crashing is all around my temples

it's a shit show alright
but i'm stumbling
out
            into the night
into
the early evening solitude

into
the no-man's-land
between
rapture and abyss

i have £5.50

in
my wallet
and one less life on the
board
but
the bars are still open
the night
is still young
and tomorrow
for all its horrors
smells sweeter than lilies

in springtime

click, click, click, click, click

yes, i have

have you ever
        sang with so much
                joy

it hurts?

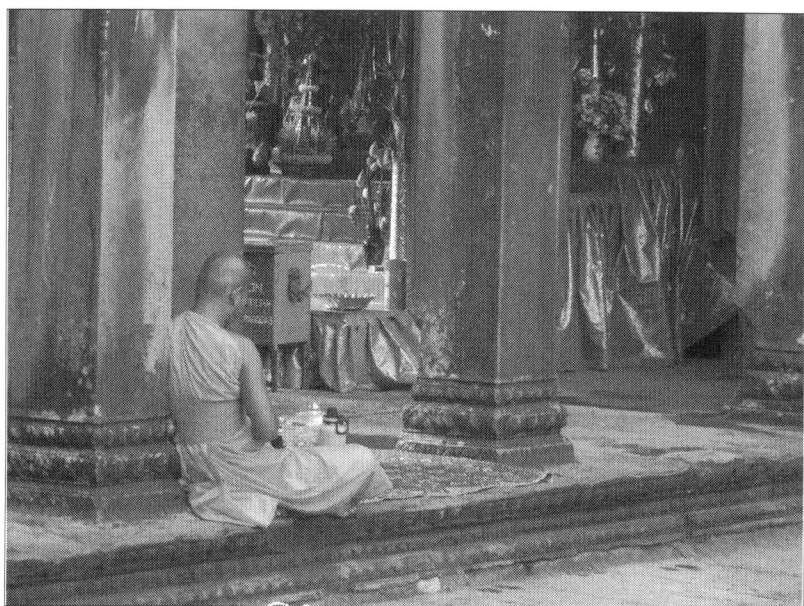

faith

lamentations on faith

I.

there is a man
who
tells me
        not
to follow
the words of an ancient desert tribe
        not
to take my own life
hostage
with a collection of books
        that are symbolic of nothing
not
to put spirituality
above science
        or knowledge
not
to answer to a being that
cannot be
        proven

II.

"believe in
humanism," he said

we are innately good

III.

death
is no unfounded rumour

rumours

IV.

death is coming

      sometimes quick, sometimes slow

"and it is finite," he says

though
they swear that death is not
          the end
just another
stop
along the way

      part of the process

V.

believe in Him
and
       you will be granted
eternal
life

VI.

i am scared of dying.

don't be

        they say

you are only returning home

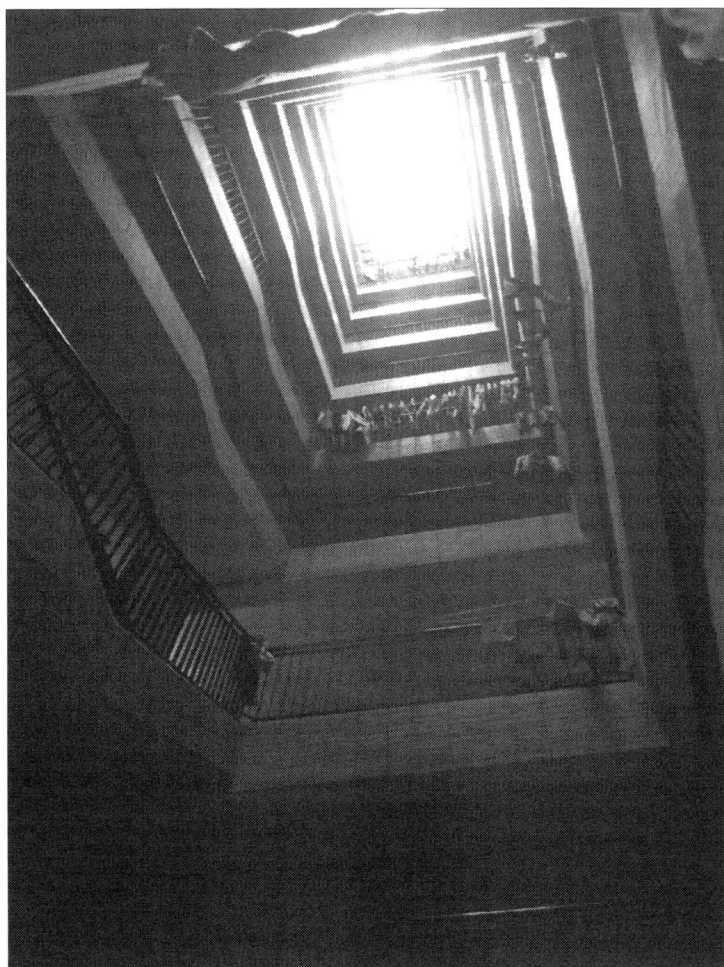

you are only returning home

VII.

"this moment
        right here
        right now

is the only meaning we will ever have"

        then he lit his smoke

VIII.

a glorious infinity
       awaits you
              they claim
if
you give yourself
to
the Lord

       hand over your love
       your understanding
       your life
             to Him;
you
will reap the rewards
in the paradise
reserved
for all believers

       for the remainder of eternity

IX.

there is
        no point

if there is no God

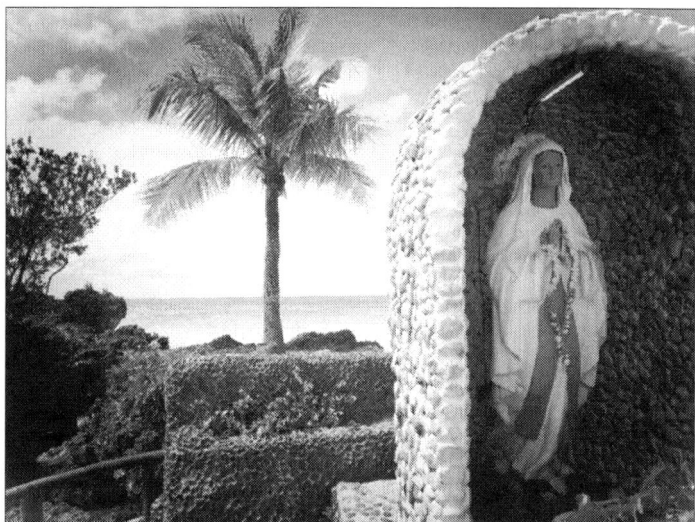

sanctity

X.

i feel the need
to
pull over onto the hard shoulder
      bleak mid-winter.

where is the meaning in my life
      if God
is nothing
but a safety net?
      a comfort blanket?
          a crutch?

who am i striking this bargain with?

XI.

don't give yourself
         to the heathens

they tell me

"don't commit yourself
         to this fantasy,"

he implores me

fantasy

XII.

God
is the creator
the
originator
the
sole innovator
the
heart-beat pulsing in the skies

let Him
        be your guide

God as creator

XIII.

i want proof

not your version
                 of the truth

XIV.

a category five hurricane struck joplin, missouri today, destroying an entire community, killing over 150 people, and flattening more than 7000 buildings; its destruction was completely indiscriminate and has left thousands of survivors homeless . . .

where was God

in all that?

XV.

"there is meaning
            in everything," he said

"you don't need myths
            to
                  create meaning"

purity

XVI.

i
stare at

      the intense lamp-light

force a sneeze.

      the relief is sublime.

where did *that* come from?

      God?

XVII.

we need

        order

        routine

        principles

        direction

without question, *you* need
        a
        relationship
            with God

XVIII.

is
my life

    a game of chance?

XIX.

we cannot
            intellectually
explain
His
        motives

            they tell me
with further
        mystery

XX.

"when you don't have any answers

                            you can't give any,"

he offers

self-assured

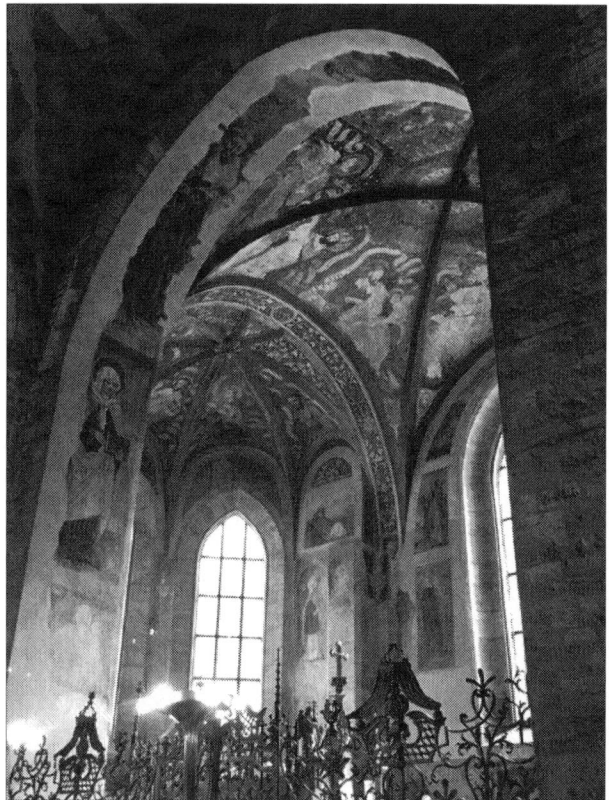

answers

XXI.

could
      it be God

raising the dust?

pushing me to demand answers?

          pressing me to question
faith?

could all this
be
    God?

on days like these

i close the curtains
turn up the heat

and wait

for something

more than this

waiting

Paul Robert Mullen

art

art
is salvation

        wherever you are from

art as salvation

the riverbank

We were just kids being kids. That's all.

Long hot summers playing down by the river, wasting time, dreaming of pretty girls. There were four of us in those days.

All I ever wanted to be when I was ten years old was a champion swimmer. You know, stood in front of a crowd with my medals held high. Honoured, confident, fit. Big muscles, bigger smile. Family looking on with pride, friends looking on with envy. That was the pinnacle of my dreams.

I *loved* to swim.

When the river was high, however, I never swam. Folks in the village told tales of missing kids in the summer drifts – how the river monsters had taken them. It rained a lot in the summer. Monsoon rains at times; the type you can barely see through or breathe in if you stand in it too long. The type of rains I used to stare at in wonder through the porch windows of the farmhouse. *Where did it come from?* It was enough to blow the mind of a kid like me. I was a good swimmer, but I wasn't too smart. Teachers said I couldn't concentrate for long; always dreaming, and imagining, and doodling in the corners of my notepad. One day I drew a river monster and the teacher snatched my pad off the desk in anger.

"See me at the end of class!"

I never did. I snuck out when some other goof was distracting her.

The rainy season here can be pretty fraught. The pathway down through the woods to the riverbank always flooded after heavy rain, and we had to wear our wellies or we'd never make it through the sludge and the mire. There were steep drops either side in parts, falling off to a certain death. Death is inconceivable as a kid, even when fear grips. I couldn't look as we shuffled past, aware of our own sensory movements like we were learning them from scratch. Fear is a funny thing. It can leave a man feeling redundant of the experience he's had all his life. The river was wide, and very beautiful to me; splitting several valleys and running down to the canyon, it was a very famous river, mother told me. She said I should be grateful to live in the palm of Mother Nature. I didn't know who Mother Nature was, but she sounded cool.

The village folk were quiet and went about their business. Most people had their jobs to do, especially the old folk, who always seemed to be pottering around with their tools and their instruments in the gardens and the square. Occasionally one would disappear; the old folk that is, and Mother said they'd been taken back to heaven to be cared for by the Lord. Very few ever came to the riverbank though. It held bad memories for some of them, Mother said, but I didn't know what she meant. River monsters only came when the river was high, they said. When the river is high, stay on the banks, they said. Grab kids playing close to the rapids by the ankles and drag them to their deaths, they said.

Then Friday 4th June, 1992, came.

His name was Robert, but we called him Bob. He was a chubby kid; always seemed to be eating something, and clumsy as hell. Candy, ice-cream, skewers of barbequed marshmallow, potato chips and popcorn. My Mother said shame on his Mother for letting him get that way, but I didn't understand what she meant. Bob was always happy and laughing with the other kids. His milk bottle thick lenses with one taped arm are still etched in my mind. His family was pretty poor. It's the one defining thing about Bob that has never left me in all these years. Years erase the important things, don't they? First it's someone's mannerisms, then it's their voice, then it's their face. Sooner or later you're only left with a name.

He was my friend, was Bob.

Bob was just Bob.

When it happened I was sat on the bank playing with my ALBA tape player. It was brand new – a birthday present from Mother – and I knew she'd worked her guts out to buy it. Had a copy of The Beatles blue album inside when I unwrapped it from its brown paper, and I'd had it on repeat ever since. You'll cost me our home in batteries, she'd said one day looking annoyed, but I didn't understand what she meant. I loved that song about a strawberry field. I could just see that place in my dreams, especially after a long day playing in the heat.

It was such a serene afternoon. There was no breeze, and the sun was so strong that everything in the distance shimmered like the reflection from a prism. Like someone was holding my eyes and shaking them real fast. In the distance we could hear the rumble of a mower cutting chess boards into the turf, and every now and then the barks from the sheepdogs on a neighbouring farm. Everything seemed so perfect, and I could feel myself growing sleepy as the late-afternoon quilt of unshaded warmth draped itself over the scene.

Something happened pretty quick. I felt it first, and then I saw it.

He lost his balance a little. The rapids had been flowing pretty fast, and Bob had stumbled out a little far towards the drift. Way further than we were ever allowed to go, even when the river was low. By the time I'd looked up he was struggling with his balance; then, in what seemed like forever, our eyes met and his laughter turned to terror. That moment went on for years, decades for me. I could see the dimples in his cheeks, the ends of his curly hair wet with sweat, and his thick eye-brows contorted around those eyes, bulging beneath twisted glasses.

Then he was gone.

The eulogy was read by Father Stevens, who was Roman Catholic and a drunk. I saw him slip himself a whiskey from a hipflask by the buffet sandwiches later that day at the wake. He had a purple nose with protruding veins, and silver hair that reflected the sun. I'd witness his own eulogy years later, in front of the biggest congregation our village had ever seen. Father Stevens taught me that drunks are not always bad people.

Mother said the eulogy Father Stevens delivered about Bob was beautiful. Captured Bob *perfectly*. I hadn't listened too closely; I was fixed on Bob's mother, hysterical, who was being held up by some other ladies I'd never seen before. They brought a coffin, but I don't think he was in it.

I never asked.

the riverbank

35

never ask me again

I.

you need your priest
        your postman
    your teacher
the world at large
    to
        believe you

you need the audience
    to applaud when the curtain rolls back

you
need to water your drinks down
    so it's not so scary;
        just
            familiar

you need to hot-wire
your thoughts
so
    the circus doesn't admit you

you need to
    think on the spot

so your life
                won't consume you
you need to inhale when
                the sunflowers wilt

you need bravery
more
                when the battle is over

you need laughter, you need joy;
                the kind that isn't shrink-wrapped
                farmed
        invented by japanese architects
                indoctrinated
                        penetrated
                                forged or manipulated

you need everything you see in
        your dreams
                to stay there, locked away
                so your days have space
        to breathe

you need sex and you need pain
and you need guilt
and you need shame
        and sometimes you must cry
                to know the true meaning of a smile

and you must take a minute
       to consider the hour

II.

don't take my words for granted
        this is not shared trauma, this is not retreat
        this has not been syphoned
                off from beat novels and pornography

        this is just *it*

pipe dreams

give me the cities
the creatures of the night
the smog and the shit and the CO_2

give me women
give me no-strings-attached
give me illicit, complicit, perverse
      the whole shebang

give me sleaze
and
corruption, and my reflection
in the shades
      of hitmen

give me 12 hour shifts
minimum wage
give me the bargains in
      dilapidated stores ran by
      immigrant families
cheap booze
      60% proof
stowaways in filthy khaki
half-eaten fried chicken bones
council houses, rough estates
      the kind you fear when darkness
            falls

give me bribery
give me starvation, degradation
state controlled emancipation
give me squalor, give me riches
chain me to this
                liberation

give me war and peace
give me inspiration
you know
            the tougher it gets
            the more the muse
                        comes with electric shocks
                        of motivation

give me marriage, adultery, divorce, murder
give me cigarettes
late night kebabs
            burnt throat whiskey deliria

give me a thumping beat
            behind Stevie Ray Vaughan
and keep giving it to me
            until the break of dawn

give me lude crosswords
and comic books
in the shadows of dangerous
                        neighbourhoods

give me
decent, open violence
    black eyes, snapped teeth, broken noses
        unnecessary beef

give me plywood walls
and tenement halls
and whores on the street
    hiding in the shadows as the bars and clubs
        pump out the big-beat

give me an aging jukebox
toothless regulars
fist fights, cocaine nights
    strobe lights
teenage sex in shop doorways before
        watching dawn climb over
    the horizon

give me fast food
    dripping in oil
give me grossly inappropriate jokes
a carton of 500 duty-free
    smokes
the politically correct dying irrepressible
    deaths
just say what you need to say
there's no time for
the rest

give me guns pressed against temples
give me humility on death row
        casinos, wild gamblers, palm-readers
           strong leaders
cement benches with drunks
                lying under damp cardboard

vicious females
          sat in lamp-lit windows
      dope dealers
alchemic healers
pills and thrills
        beautiful, untouched drudgery

give me days and days and days
      in bed –
          sometimes
you've just got to give it all up
take a spacer, refuel
self-medicate with an explosion of
                isolation

give me lady macbeth in her wicked glory
          pornography
give me 3.30am, bangs in the dark
give me bedsits
liquor stores, hangovers
cheap whores

give me Andy Warhol's fetishes
give me Einstein's brains
give me 4D rollercoasters with the g-force
      of a fighter jet
give them back their freedom
           on the great plains
give me factories, fatalities, cheddar cheese

strangers in cubicles
           on their knees

give me second hand cars, give me crippling fear
bittersweet landladies
ugliness
      unruliness
give me Henry Miller
give me gruesome history
give me nasty dogs
      with tattooed owners
give me thorn bushes, fake money
      negative equity
give me twisted roadkill
the tortured soul at the piano
the rich and the poor
           in a pit with fists
give me cyanide
      in the courtroom
give me blowjobs
      in the locker room

give me bone-crunching injustice
torture for those
        hell-bent on prejudice

give me
thunder crackling along the track
give me nothing
        but a rucksack on
                my back

give me the fool
        don't give me the king

give me fleeting glory; that, at least
        is more satisfying
        than permanent obscurity

give me saturated fat
salt, msg, e-numbers
        sugar, sugar, sugar
give me all the advice in the world –
        i'll trash it with the poisoned roaches
                and rotting meat
        i'll trample it with my dancing
                feet
give me the opposite of what's going on
give me tension
        on the way to breaking even
give me UFO's, give me nudity

give me french fries trembling in fat
give me unreasonable, graceless
                    gluttony

give me guy fawkes, robin hood
give me Beckett and Celine
give me all the tea in china
            give me F. Scott Fitzgerald's
                    american dream

give me strangers
            in the night
        give me Martin Luther King
give me anxious laughter
give me the insanity
        that being pinned down
                and tickled against your will
                    brings

give me poets working endlessly
give me laughter in the cemetery
give me
        all the tools i'll ever need
                    to be free
just give it all to *me*

give me voodoo, witchcraft, poltergeists and crazy dreams
give me saints and sinners
            losers and winners

lost souls ripped apart
      at the seams

give me slide guitar
      in an empty concert hall
give me the wise man just days from death
      and that flick of his brow
            that says it all
give me
the typecast resurrected
      give me a lock of your hair
scattered ashes on the road to nowhere
the clinically disturbed
the champion unnerved
      the pretty girl
      in the mood for a melody
the reclusive icon
      on street corners in disguise
the leader of the free world
with no alibis

      broken hearts healing
however long it takes
sweet souls departed
      returning to take a break
give me clergymen lost in time
give me lady Macbeth again
      burning in the bowels of hell

give me enlightenment in the darkest corners
give me faith and all its rewards
give me heavy metal
       give me endless, glorious
            minor chords

give me earthquakes
       and let me shake
give me absolutely
          no escape

now there's a thought
               i guess i'll wait

give me the cities

dark places

6 minutes
until
> my 35th birthday
and
the shit-storm
is
> bubbling
in minds all over town

my dream is gone
> like
the village underneath the
> volcano
drowned
in ash and silt and fire
but
> my spirit is ready to fly
to
far flung lands
where
women dance in the streets
to the tune
> of every living
> heartbeat

and
the wars

of a thousand generations
      lie
dormant
until the revolving door
of history
         sweeps in that catalyst

that changes

    *every*thing

dark places

sparks

to all those who have died
making love
or
gripping the bar
> like a roller-coaster

i salute you

sparks

poetry for fools

i am penniless
with a trunk full of yellowing manuscripts
and useless recollections
of that
mosquito-ridden boat
through the jungles of borneo-
darkness on the swamps
and stars
      in my eyes

there are apparitions
in my mind

murder is damnation
and so much work, too;
      i can see
the effigies of brooding souls
written on the rocks
beside the roads
leading to the fires
      on the highways of the world

i am over-sexed
      and underwhelmed

there is so much life in
these towns
that i pass through –
so much tenderness, so much isolation

the burden of one's days:
isolation.

it's hard
to appreciate the dawn
to lie on your back basking on the
beaches of the sub-tropics
to return to the body after cataclysmic
animalistic orgasm
to walk the railroads with
a high-school love
to sit on park benches as newlyweds
push future leaders, murderers, game-changers
past in gifted strollers
to simply exist in this moment
when
isolation burns like bodies

in a crematorium

it's true

even white girls
                get the blues
the rich ones too
lowdown
        in their privileged
        hue

and sometimes
no amount of gin
or fingers, tongues or cocks within
        can take the blues
        away

they end up front page news
or wasting away
        in a vortex of cheap speed
        and booze
trapped in the shadows of late-night dives
        waiting for another
        lonely ride
into the darkening rain
back to square one
or
    worse;
            to an empty bed

where dreams
fester, caught in webs
eight legs staring

twitching
                waiting

back to square one

freedom

take flight

spread your wings

never look back

there's music to be made

somewhere

*any*where

freedom

the accumulation of the sexes

for as long as there are
mountains standing
proud
in tibet, i will never understand
the death
                of romance
in that
frozen, epitaphic agony
        that
we deal ourselves
by
        our own hand

it's that strobe-light encore
on a night
you've waited for
all your life

        before

                the lights come up

the end

i'm going to end this collection here
you see, it feels like
i'm just
clutching at straws

bent over
       wordless
              on all fours

i've nothing left to say today
so, i'm going to hand
it over
       to you

let's just say
       the stage is yours . . .

the stage is yours

time passes so quickly . . . all we ever have is *now*

acknowledgements

This is an important collection for me, both personally and creatively. My waking minutes, hours, days, weeks and months have been spent contemplating this project. I'd like to thank Frances Moxley Zinder for her evenings on a third floor, Chinese balcony, and in a Burmese hotel room, tea in hand, listening, discussing, and encouraging with interest. I'd like to thank Kate Evans for her editing whizz, constant inspiration and poetic companionship. As always, Jan McCutcheon for her design, editing, patience and vision. Also to Heyans Shukla for his patience, negotiating skills, and commitment to helping me during my editing dramas in India.

*

Thank you to my family and friends who tolerate my eccentricities, and have helped and enabled me to reach 35 with such freedom.

*

This is the age of the camera phone, and therefore gems are captured in situations where, in the past, we may only have reminisced. It is a new art form to be admired.

*

Thank you firstly to the hugely talented Caleb Wilkinson (www.flickr.com/calebandhobbes) & (www.instagram.com/nationkb) for his outstanding front cover photo, plus other inventive, unique images.

*

Thank you to the extremely artistic Darshan Mahida (www.instagram.com/darsh_mahida) & (www.facebook.com/Digitaleye photography17), and the equally imaginative Ankit Mavchi (www.instagram.com/qrious35mm) & (www.ankitmavchi.com) for their professional contributions.

*

Also, great thanks to Kerrie Henderson, Jonathan Tudor, Daria Romanov, Luke Rimmer, Yaroslav Alexandrovski, Cathy Birdsong Dutchak, Adrien Noël, Kelly Sykes, Lei Li Xian, Matthew Teske, Santiago Amaya, Frances Moxley Zinder, Hermansius Nordi, Dave Rhine, Gerry Parenti, Paul Kappa, Derek Sykes, and Joe Davies for their photo contributions.

*

Thank you also to model Poojah Desai (www.instagram.com/poojadesai) for her permission to include her image.

*

I am thrilled to say that France, China, Russia, U.S.A, Canada, India, Italy, Indonesia, Colombia, and the U.K are represented amongst my friends, the photographers.

*

Thanks to all who have bought my work, and who support little known poets.

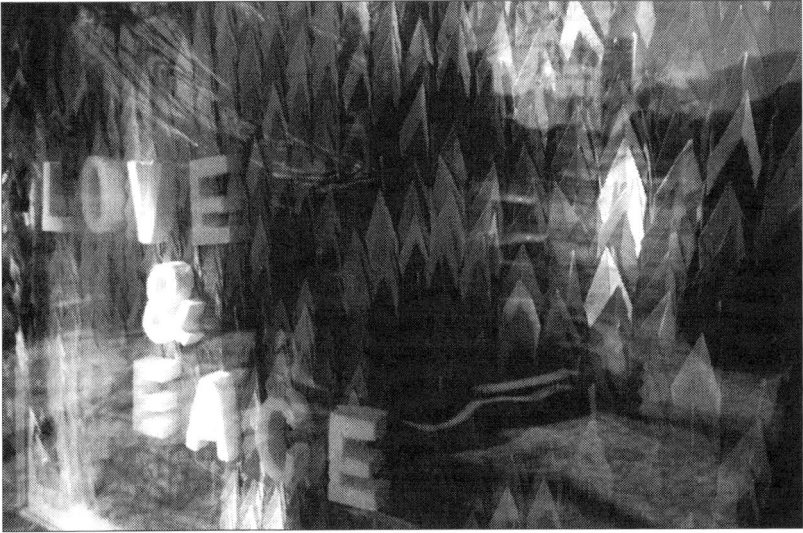

love & peace

Paul Robert Mullen was born in Southport, near Liverpool, England, in 1982. He is a writer, musician, and university lecturer, currently taking a hiatus in various parts of the world. His poetry has been widely published in a variety of literary journals, magazines and e-zines. He is also an avid blogger.

He is the author of *curse this blue raincoat* (2017) and *testimony* (2018).

www.paulrobertmullen.com

photo credits

primitive cool, Nanning, China, 2013 © Matthew Teske

crossroads in winter, Leicester Square, London, England, 2018 © Kelly Sykes

you, Pooja Desai in Surat, Gujarat, India, 2017 © Darshan Mahida,

early morning sun, Crosby, Liverpool, England, 2012 © Jonathan Tudor

burn, Koh Lanta, Thailand, 2018 © Gerry Parenti

curious at the very least, Vientiane, Laos, 2017 © Paul Robert Mullen

grace, Bali, Indonesia, 2017 © Daria Romanov

voluntary exit, Qingyuan, China, 2012 © Kerrie Henderson

wanderlust, Vientiane, Laos, 2017 © Paul Robert Mullen

maybe we will walk the corridors of the future together, Pyongyang University, North Korea, 2017 © Paul Robert Mullen

pariah, Surat, Gujarat, India, 2016 © Ankit Mavchi

constant craving, Boracay, Phillipines, 2018 © Paul Robert Mullen

erudition, Gold Coast, Australia, 2017 © Joe Davies

give me the cities, Hong Kong, 2009 © Adrien Noël

dark places, Nanning, China, 2015 © Caleb Wilkinson

sparks, Tomsk, Russia, 2018 © Yaroslav Alexandrovski

back to square one, Nanning, China, 2015 © Caleb Wilkinson

freedom, Macau, 2015 © Luke Rimmer

the stage is yours, Maafushi Island, Maldives, 2014 © Santiago Amaya

boracay, Boracay, Phillipines, 2018 © Paul Robert Mullen

love & peace, Hiroshima, Japan, 2015 © Paul Robert Mullen

Printed in Great Britain
by Amazon